CH

palm reading

Mind Games

ARE YOU PSYCHIC?

Facts, Trivia, and Quizzes

fortune-teller

Elsie Olson

Lerner Publications ◆ Minneapolis

Lerner Publications Company
A division of Lerner Publishing Group, Inc.
241 First Avenue North
Minneapolis, MN 55401 USA

For reading levels and more information, look up this title at www.lernerbooks.com.

Main body text set in Avenir LT Pro
Typeface provided by Linotype

Library of Congress Cataloging-in-Publication Data

The Cataloging-in-Publication Data for *Are You Psychic?* is on file at the Library of Congress.
ISBN 978-1-5124-3416-3 (lib. bdg.)
ISBN 978-1-5124-4937-2 (EB pdf)

Manufactured in the United States of America
1-42052-23922-2/22/2017

CONTENTS

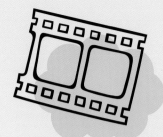

Introduction

UNLEASH YOUR INNER PSYCHIC

It's Sunday morning, and your day is wide open. You think about calling your best friend to ask if he wants to go see a movie. Suddenly, your phone buzzes. Your best friend sent a text: "Want to catch a movie?" It's as if he was reading your mind! **Coincidence** or **psychic** connection?

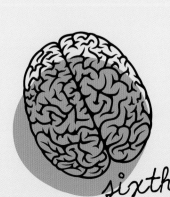

sixth sense

SIXTH SENSE

Many people believe they have special abilities that give them a sixth sense. A sixth sense can include the ability to know things that would be impossible to know by normal use of the senses. This is called extra-sensory perception (ESP). It can also include mind reading and **predicting** the future.

FACT OR FICTION?

Most scientists say psychic abilities can be explained by coincidence or tricks. Still, many people believe in a sixth sense. Whether real or imagined, exploring psychic abilities can be a lot of fun. Could you be a psychic? Read on and find out!

extra-sensory perception

Chapter 1
ANCIENT ESP

People have believed in psychic abilities for thousands of years. Prophets, **seers**, and fortune-tellers were common in many ancient civilizations. Many of these psychics practiced divination, which is **foretelling** the future.

ASK THE ORACLE

In ancient Greece, people visited a famous **oracle**. The oracle would go into a **trance** and say strange words. Greeks believed these words could reveal the future.

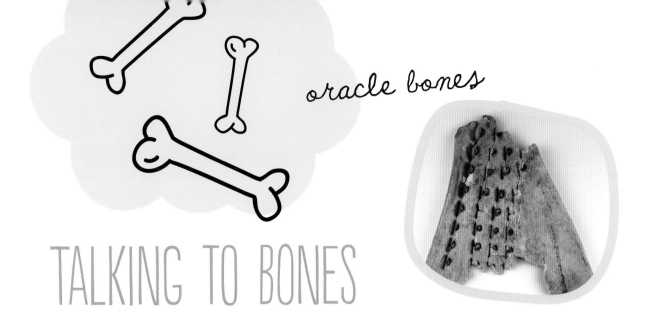

oracle bones

TALKING TO BONES

In ancient China, diviners predicted the future using bones from dead animals. The diviner applied heat to a bone while asking it questions. The heat caused the bone to crack. The diviner then interpreted the cracks to answer the questions.

SPIRIT SACRIFICES

In western Africa, people practiced the religion Vodun. They believed Vodun priests could influence the future. They made sacrifices, such as food or drink, to spirits. They hoped this would persuade the spirits to help the living.

Chapter 2
SCIENCE AND PSYCHICS

For thousands of years, divination was a part of religion, not science. This changed in 1882 when the Society for Psychical Research was founded in England. This group applied scientific investigation to the paranormal. It wanted to expose fake psychics.

PSYCHIC TESTS

Throughout the 1900s, many other groups performed tests on people claiming to be psychics. Some tests used a computer to **randomly** display images. The person being tested had to guess what image would appear. If they guessed correctly often enough, they were thought to be psychic.

CRIME AND SPIES

Psychic abilities have never been scientifically proven. But many people still believe in a sixth sense. Psychics have found work helping law enforcement solve cases. And the US government has said it has used psychics to help with spying.

mind reading

COOL OR COINCIDENCE?

Most scientists believe psychic visions are just a coincidence. There are more than seven billion people on Earth. With so many people having thoughts, dreams, and ideas, some are going to match true events.

BODY LANGUAGE

Some scientists believe people who claim to be psychics are able to pick up **subtle** body language cues. These people can guess the way someone is feeling based on these movements. This can seem a lot like mind reading, but most people could be taught this skill. Still, it is very difficult to prove that psychic powers do *not* exist!

How Psychic Are You?

Do you have any psychic abilities? Take the test below to find out. Write your answers on a separate sheet of paper. Can you guess what your results will be?

ANSWER YES OR NO:

1. Have you ever correctly guessed the next song on the radio?

2. Have you and a friend ever said the exact same thing at the exact same time?

3. Have you ever gotten goose bumps for seemingly no reason?

4. Have you ever felt a special connection with an animal?

5. Do you follow your gut when making hard decisions?

6. Do you remember your dreams most nights?

7. Have you ever met someone for the first time but could have sworn you've met them before?

8. Do your friends and family call you lucky?

9. Do you ever feel like something good or bad is about to happen?

10. Have you ever had a dream that seemed to come true?

Tally your answers. Give yourself two points for each yes and one point for each no.

18–20: No crystal ball needed. You're a super psychic!

14–17: You're a bit psychic. But don't put too much faith in your predictions!

10–13: You haven't tapped into your psychic powers yet, but keep trying!

Are You and Your Bestie Psychic Soul Mates?

Take this quiz with a friend to find out if you share a spooky psychic connection. Concentrate very hard on what your friend is thinking as you answer. Write down your answers on separate sheets of paper. No peeking! Then compare your results.

1. Think of a number between one and five.

2. Which animal pair best represents you and your bestie?

   A.

   B.

   C.

3. Which fictional friends best represent you and your bestie?

   A. Ron Weasley and Harry Potter

   B. Pikachu and Ash

   C. C-3PO and R2-D2

4. Pick a color.

   A.

   B.

   C.

   D.

5. Pick a shape.

   A.

   B.

   C.

   D.

6. **What song best represents you and your bestie?**

7. **What food best represents you and your bestie?**

A.

B.

C.

8. **What do you see in this picture?**

9. **What is your favorite moment that you and your bestie have shared?**

10. **Pick a vacation.**

A.

B.

C.

Compare your answers with your friend's. How many matched up?

1–3: Great minds don't always think alike! You and your bestie do not share a psychic connection, but you still make a great team.

4–7: You and your bestie definitely think alike. Coincidence or special connection?

8–10: You and your bestie are of one mind. You always know what the other is thinking!

Chapter 3

POWERS OF THE MIND

Many psychic abilities are related to odd things people believe they can do with their minds. Have you ever tried to send a message using your mind? This is called telepathy. It is communicating without using the five senses.

TWIN TELEPATHY

Some people think twins can communicate telepathically. But scientists argue that twins just know each other very well. They share many life experiences and are able to pick up on subtle cues from one another that others may not notice.

déjà vu

It's True!

Have you ever felt that you've experienced something for a second time? This is déjà vu! As many as seventy percent of people say they have had this feeling.

YOU ARE GETTING VERY SLEEPY

Mind control, **brainwashing**, and zombies might sound like science fiction. But have you ever watched a **hypnotist**? You were seeing mind control at work! Hypnotists put their subjects into a very relaxed state of mind. In this state, people's imaginations are very strong. So, if a hypnotist suggests something, it can feel very real.

UP IN FLAMES

Some psychics claim they can start something on fire just by looking at it! This is known as pyrokinesis. There is no proof of anyone ever using pyrokinesis. But it is still a popular psychic superpower in books and movies!

It's True!

Can your dog read your mind? Many people have reported dogs acting strangely when their owners were injured in a different location. Science hasn't proven that dogs are mind readers. But studies have shown dogs are better at picking up on human body language than any other animal.

mind reader

Chapter 4
OBJECT CONTROL

Many psychics claim to have amazing powers when it comes to objects. Some believe objects can pass along information. Others believe they can use their mind to make objects move.

MIND MUSCLE

The ability to move or control objects is known as telekinesis. It includes bending, lifting, or even throwing objects without touching them. Many people throughout history have claimed to have this ability. But most were proven to be fakes.

telekinesis

THING HISTORY

Some psychics believe that every object has a story to tell. They learn this story by holding an object and concentrating. For example, by holding a lost mitten, the psychic says they learn who owned the mitten. This is known as psychometry.

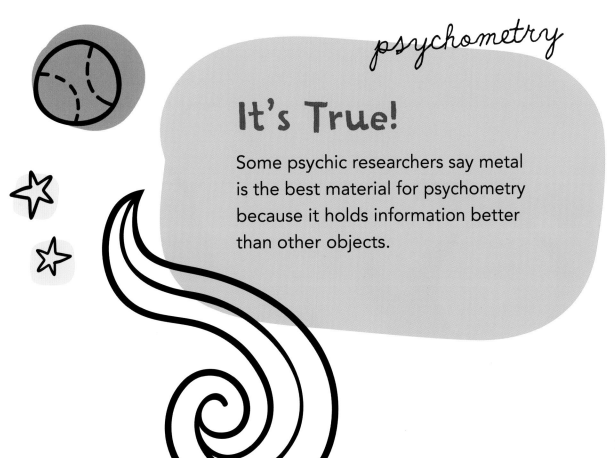

psychometry

It's True!

Some psychic researchers say metal is the best material for psychometry because it holds information better than other objects.

Chapter 5

SEEING IS BELIEVING

Has a fortune-teller ever predicted your future? Have you ever felt that something was going to happen, and then it did? Both of these are said to be clairvoyance, the knowledge of events learned using unusual means.

CRYSTAL BALLS

Some psychics use crystal balls to predict the future. This is called scrying. Psychics gaze into the ball, looking for shapes in the crystal. They say these shapes inspire images in their minds that tell of the future.

fortune-teller

TEA TIME

Other psychics study the leaves left over after someone drinks a cup of loose-leaf tea. They believe the shapes they find in these leaves can tell of the tea drinker's past, present, and future.

WRITTEN IN THE CARDS

Tarot cards are another psychic tool. Each deck has 78 cards. Each card has a different image. The tarot reader shuffles the deck and lays some or all of the cards face-up in a pattern. Then they interpret the meaning of the cards. This tells them about a person's life and future.

In the Palm of Your Hand

Palm reading is one of the most common forms of psychic prediction. Look at your hand. See the lines? Palm readers study these lines. They believe the lines reveal details about a person's personality and life.

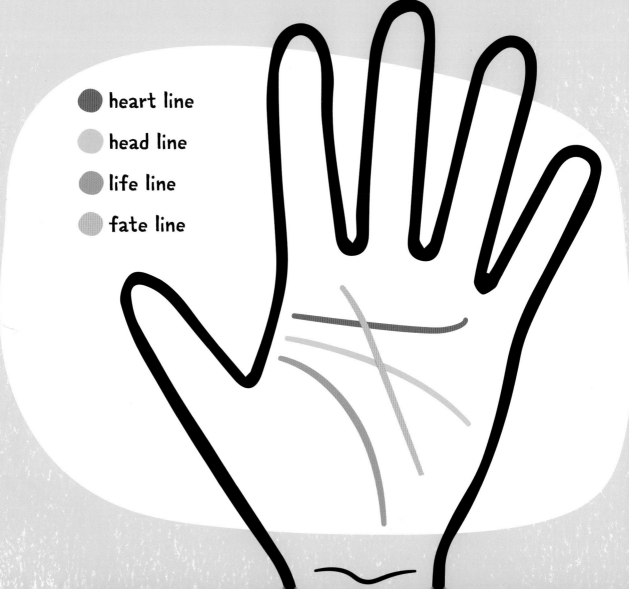

- heart line
- head line
- life line
- fate line

What Kind of Friend Are You?

The heart line is one of the most important lines for palm readers. They believe this line tells of your personality and your relationships with others. Compare your heart line to the pictures below to find out what kind of friend you are!

IF YOU HAVE A:

Long, straight heart line: The Considerate Pal.
You are a logical thinker. You are always aware of others' feelings.

Short, straight line: The Doer. You like alone time and don't always follow the pack. You express your feelings with actions rather than words.

Long, curved line: The Party Animal. You are social and always up for fun. Your emotions often guide your decisions.

Short, curved line: The True-Blue Buddy. You can seem shy at first, but you are a great friend! You prefer small groups to crowds.

Broken or split heart line: The Giver. You always put your friends' needs first.

VISIONS AND DREAMS

Some clairvoyants don't need any tools. They simply have visions. These visions can appear when the psychic is awake or when he or she is dreaming.

PSYCHIC PROS

Many psychics turn their amazing abilities into a career. People come to them looking for answers about their lives. Professional psychics may use scrying, tarot cards, palm reading, or other tools during these visits. Many people find that visiting a psychic can give them a new way of looking at their life.

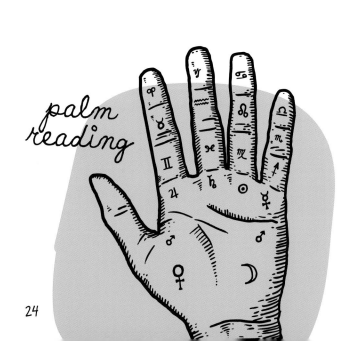

palm reading

It's True!

US president Woodrow Wilson visited a psychic. Psychic Edgar Cayce gave Wilson guidance during his presidency.

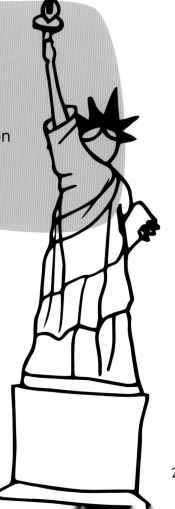

Chapter 6

PSYCHIC YOU!

Can psychic readings tell your future? Could you be a psychic? Since science has not proven or disproven psychic powers, it is up to you to decide! Whether psychic abilities are fact or faction, they are fun to learn about. They could even tell you something about yourself!

psychic readings

EXPLORE MORE!

Psychic readings are just one way people learn more about themselves. They also use astrology, dream interpretation, and more. Have fun exploring matters of the mind. Soon you will be an expert in you!

Psychic Card Creation!

In addition to tarot cards, psychics use Zener cards. These are decks of 25 cards used to test and practice psychic abilities. Make your own set to see how psychic you are!

Materials:

- several sheets of card stock
- ruler
- pencil
- scissors
- markers or crayons
- sheet of paper

Step 1: Use a ruler to draw twenty-five rectangles on the card stock. Each should be about 2 inches (5 centimeters) by 3 inches (7.6 cm).

Step 2: Cut the cards out.

Step 3: Draw the following shapes on each of five cards: +, O, □, ≈, ☆. Use different colors for each shape.

Step 4: Repeat step 3 until you have five cards for each shape. Make all similar shapes the same color. For example, make all circles blue and all squares red.

Step 5: Decide who will be the sender and who will be the subject. The subject will try to guess the cards. The sender will look at the cards.

Step 6: Have the sender shuffle the cards. Then, the sender should flip the first one up and look at it, but not show the subject. The subject should concentrate and try to guess the card. On a separate sheet of paper, the sender records a point for each guess the subject gets right.

Step 7: Repeat step 6 until you have gone through the entire deck. Then switch sender and subject roles.

Step 8: Keep track of all results. The higher your score, the more psychic you are!

GLOSSARY

brainwashing: forcing someone to either give up beliefs or accept different beliefs by using various means of mental pressure

coincidence: an occurrence of events that happen by accident but seem to have some sort of connection

foretelling: telling of the future

hypnotist: a person who studies hypnosis, or the practice of putting people into a state in which they appear to be sleeping but can still see, hear, and respond to suggestions and questions

oracle: a person through whom a god is believed to speak, and who gives wise answers or opinions about the future

predicting: saying what will happen in the future

psychic: seeming or claiming to be sensitive to nonphysical or supernatural forces

randomly: created or occurring without order or purpose

seers: people who claim to see the future by practicing divination, especially by concentrating on a glass or crystal ball

subtle: not strong or obvious

trance: a mental state in which a person is conscious but not really aware of what is happening around him or her

FURTHER INFORMATION

How to Do a Simple Number Mind Trick

http://www.wikihow.com/Do-a-Simple-Number-Mind-Trick

You may not be a mind reader, but follow the instructions at this website to learn how to fool your friends into thinking you are!

Math Magic Tricks

http://www.pbs.org/parents/adventures-in-learning/2015/01/math-magic-tricks

Use the power of math to read a friend's mind and perform other amazing magic tricks.

Moore, Gareth. *Not So Ordinary*. Minneapolis, MN: Hungry Tomato, 2016.

Stretch your mind and test your powers of deductions with the activities in this book.

Owings, Lisa. *ESP*. Minneapolis, MN: Bellwether Media, Inc., 2015.

Are psychic powers real? Read this book and decide for yourself!

Perish, Patrick. *Is ESP Real?* Mankato, MN: Amicus, 2014.

Examine the evidence to find out if extra-sensory perception is fact or fiction.

INDEX

Photo Acknowledgments

The images in this book are used with the permission of: Design elements and doodles © balabolka/Shutterstock.com, Daria Rosen/Shutterstock.com, Fears/Shutterstock.com, josep perianes jorba/Shutterstock.com, mhatzapa/Shutterstock.com, Mighty Media, Inc., Mjosedesign/Shutterstock.com, Naatali/Shutterstock.com, Nikolaeva/Shutterstock.com, Photoraidz/Shutterstock.com, primiaou/Shutterstock.com, Sashatigar/Shutterstock.com, studioworkstock/Shutterstock.com, Vector Tradition/Shutterstock.com, and whitemomo/Shutterstock.com; © mediaphotos/iStockphoto.com, p. 1 (top, left); © Kerfluffle/iStockphoto.com, pp. 1 (top, right), 24 (left); © Ollyy/Shutterstock.com, p. 1 (bottom); © Monkey Business Images/Shutterstock.com, p. 3; © JBryson/iStockphoto.com, p. 4 (top); © adriaticfoto/Shutterstock.com, p. 4 (bottom); © master1305/iStockphoto.com, p. 5; © Bibi Saint-Pol/Wikimedia Commons, p. 6; © British Library/Wikimedia Commons, p. 7; © Fertnig/iStockphoto.com, p. 8; © Uber Images/Shutterstock.com, p. 9; © ptasha/iStockphoto.com, p. 10; © mixetto/iStockphoto.com, p. 11; © Dar_ria/iStockphoto.com, p. 12 (fox and wolf); © MirasWonderland/Shutterstock.com, p. 12 (dog and cat); © Rimma Zaynagova/Shutterstock.com, p. 12 (otter and owl); © Oldrich/Shutterstock.com, p. 12 (Ron Weasley and Harry Potter); © enchanted_fairy/Shutterstock.com, p. 12 (Pikachu and Ash); © Featureflash Photo Agency/Shutterstock.com, p. 12 (C-3PO and R2-D2); © Macrovector/Shutterstock.com, p. 13 (bacon and eggs); © gst/Shutterstock.com, p. 13 (peanut butter and jelly sandwich); © Rvector/Shutterstock.com, p. 13 (apple and oranges); © Veronika Kokurina/Shutterstock.com, p. 13 (dog or cats optical illusion); © dibrova/Shutterstock.com, p. 13 (beach); © FamVeld/Shutterstock.com, p. 13 (child skiing); © Ultima_Gaina/iStockphoto.com, p. 13 (city skyline); © Maica/iStockphoto.com, p. 14; © GlobalStock/iStockphoto.com, p. 15; © Juanmonino/iStockphoto.com, p. 16; © carebott/iStockphoto.com, p. 17; © JGI/Jamie Grill/Thinkstockphotos.com, p. 19; © turk_stock_photographer/Thinkstockphotos.com, p. 20; © ellenamani/iStockphoto.com, p. 21; © DigitalFabiani/Shutterstock.com, p. 24 (right); © Harris & Ewing/Library of Congress/Wikimedia Commons, p. 25 (top); © Everett Collection/Shutterstock.com, p. 25 (bottom); © ANURAK PONGPATIMET/Shutterstock.com, p. 26; © Monika Wisniewska/Shutterstock.com, p. 27 (top); © diane39/iStockphoto.com, p. 27 (bottom); © SerrNovik/Thinkstockphotos.com, p. 29; © vm/iStockphoto.com, p. 31.

Front cover: © mediaphotos/iStockphoto.com (top); © monkeybusinessimages/iStockphoto.com (left); © Monkey Business Images/Shutterstock.com (middle, top); © Photographee.eu/Shutterstock.com (middle, bottom); © Kerfluffle/iStockphoto.com (middle, hand drawing); © Ollyy/Shutterstock.com (right).

Back cover: © master1305/iStockphoto.com (left); © GlobalStock/iStockphoto.com (right).